PENNY PRAYERS
TRUE STORIES OF CHANGE

MARION AMBERG

Liguori
LIGUORI, MISSOURI

Imprimi Potest:
Harry Grile, CSsR, Provincial
Denver Province, The Redemptorists

Published by Liguori Publications
Liguori, Missouri 63057

To order, call 800-325-9521
www.liguori.org

Copyright © 2014 Marion Amberg

All rights reserved. No part of this publication may be reproduced, stored in a retrieval system, or transmitted in any form or by any means—electronic, mechanical, photocopy, recording, or any other—except for brief quotations in printed reviews, without the prior written permission of Liguori Publications.

Library of Congress Cataloging-in-Publication Data

Amberg, Marion.
 Penny prayers : true stories of change : / Marion Amberg.—First Edition.
    pages cm
 1. Prayer—Christianity. 2. Trust in God—Christianity.
 3. Mottoes—United States. I. Title.
 BV220.A4155 2014
 242—dc23

2013030590

p ISBN: 978-0-7648-2392-3

e ISBN: 978-0-7648-6878-8

Scripture texts in this work are taken from the *New American Bible*, revised edition © 2010, 1991, 1986, 1970 Confraternity of Christian Doctrine, Washington, D.C., and are used by permission of the copyright owner. All Rights Reserved. No part of the *New American Bible* may be reproduced in any form without permission in writing from the copyright owner.

Liguori Publications, a nonprofit corporation, is an apostolate of The Redemptorists. To learn more about The Redemptorists, visit Redemptorists.com.

Printed in the United States of America
18 17 16 15 14 / 5 4 3 2 1
First Edition

Dedication

*To my mother
—and to all the mothers of her generation—
who could stretch a penny
from here to eternity.*

Acknowledgments

A "cent-imental" thank you to everyone who contributed their penny stories for this book. "In God We Trust" proclaims the penny above Lincoln's bust, and your stories are filled with trust, inspiration, and humor. May heaven send you even more pennies and penny tales from above!

I also extend my heartfelt appreciation to the penny pray-ers—especially the Carmelite nuns of Santa Fe, New Mexico—who supported this book endeavor on their knees. Your presence in my life is no "coin-incidence."

Ending where this book began, I express my deepest gratitude to *St. Anthony Messenger* for publishing my *Penny Prayer* story in its February 2009 issue. When readers began responding with their own penny stories, I realized the phrase "In God We Trust" is more than our nation's motto—it is a growing prayer movement of trusting in the divine!

Note: Stories in this book, though told in third person, are firsthand accounts of individuals and their encounters with pennies, as well as their experience with the penny prayer.

Contents

Chapter One
Pennies of Provision:
In God We Trust for Our Life Needs **1**

Chapter Two
Pennies of Guidance:
In God We Trust for Direction in Life **19**

Chapter Three
Pennies From Heaven:
In God We Trust for Deceased Loved Ones **49**

Chapter Four
Pennies of Spirituality:
In God We Trust to Increase Our Faith **69**

Chapter Five
Penny Drives:
In God We Trust for Impossible Projects **81**

Foreword

The Author's Penny Story

What good is a penny? It has the power to answer prayers!

I've always picked up pennies wherever I found them—in parking lots, on sidewalks, even in front of a church. I'm not necessarily a penny pincher, but there's something "cent-sational" about finding a penny. Maybe it's because I feel blessed, or because it's a penny I didn't have to earn.

One day when I found a penny lying on a sidewalk, I didn't shove it into my pocket as usual. I brushed it off, then fingered the raised surfaces and studied the coin. "D" was for Denver, where the coin was minted in 1985. No longer shiny, the penny was beginning to tarnish from the many hands that had touched it over the years.

I felt just like the coin: tarnished from the hand that life had dealt me. I had a leg injury that doctors said was irreversible. I was experiencing financial worries and needed to make crucial decisions about my future. *Should I do this or do that?* I turned the coin over and discovered a message worth more than all the riches of the world.

"In God We Trust," proclaimed tiny capital letters above the bust of Abraham Lincoln, the sixteenth president of the United States. Prompted by an inner nudge, I prayed, "God, I trust in you." Immediately a sense of calm and peace descended on me like a warm blanket. The next time I found a penny, I repeated the prayer.

Finding pennies and praying the penny prayer became a kind of spiritual high for me. Whether I was out walking for exercise or running an errand, I would inspect anything that was round and about the size of a penny. One "old penny" turned out to be a wad of well-used gum! I've dug out pennies frozen in snow and ice and pried them loose from hot tarred streets. Some pennies were dirtier than sin, but I picked them up anyway. Cleaning away the dirt as though I were cleaning my own soul, I prayed, "God, I trust in you."

My financial and other worries didn't disappear like magic, but that simple prayer helped me to trust in God's plans for my life. And whenever I need reassurance of God's providence, more pennies from heaven seem to land in my path.

A penny and a prayer: It sounds too simple, but the physical act of holding up a penny and declaring my trust in God lifts burdens from me. When I take back my problems—as we all sometimes do—I find another penny and recommit my trust in the Almighty.

So find a penny and say the penny prayer—then watch for change in your life!

Several of Marion Amberg's stories in this book, as well as Rita Waldref's testimony, were adapted from Marion's article "Penny Prayers," published in the February 2009 issue of St. Anthony Messenger.

PENNY PRAYERS
TRUE STORIES OF CHANGE

Chapter One

Pennies of Provision: In God We Trust for Our Life Needs

"Give us this day our daily bread," we ask our heavenly Father in the Lord's Prayer. Though our "daily bread" indeed means food and drink, it also represents other life needs—such as the need for a job or money to fill the gas tank, or even the humorous need of a prankster-friar. As the penny stories in this chapter testify, heaven loves to meet our needs—all we have to do is ask and trust.

Pennies for the Christ Child

There's joy in giving—even pennies. That's the lesson the author of this book learned one Christmastide.

Just two weeks before Christmas one year, Marion Amberg was shocked to learn her job would be terminated. Making ends meet was already tough, and she wondered where she'd find another job in the worsening economy. During Mass on Christmas morning, she dropped all her pennies—and her worries—in the collection plate.

"God, I trust in you," she silently prayed, feeling like the poor drummer boy in the Christmas carol who played his drum because that's all he had to offer the Christ Child.

Marion's gift to God came back to her. Several days later her job was reinstated for a couple more months, giving her time to find other employment.

"It's a Christmas I'll never forget," Marion said. "I trusted, and God answered—in the most unexpected way!"

The Penny Rx

Like laughter, a penny can be good medicine, especially when it's "heaven-cent."

One day, Roberto Gonzales of Albuquerque, New Mexico, was picking up twelve prescriptions at his pharmacy. When the clerk handed Roberto his tall stack of medicines, he noticed the receipt for the prescription on top read $180. "That was for just one drug!" exclaimed Roberto. The clerk then noticed one bottle of meds was missing and went to retrieve it.

"She left before I could tell her to cancel the $180 prescription because I couldn't afford it," continued Roberto, who is widely known for his religious folk art. "I had no insurance."

At that very moment, as though it were preordained, Roberto looked down and saw a shiny penny lying on the floor. "I picked it up and read 'In God We Trust,'" he said. The clerk returned with the missing bottle and said the drug was now available in generic form. Would he prefer the generic drug for $16 rather than $180?

Roberto looked at the penny and smiled. "I'll take the generic," he said, his heart skipping a beat at the wonder of it all.

"On the way home, I pondered what might have happened to my health if I hadn't found the penny and God's timely message. I had planned to cancel the prescription because of the exorbitant price."

A penny Rx from heaven—just what the divine Doctor ordered!

The Power of "Change"

Can spare change be a part of God's plan? Yes, if it helps you trust in God! That's the story of Richard and Jane Wong of northern New Mexico, whose names have been changed at their request.

In the early 1980s, the couple was living in California and had just turned forty years old when they converted to Catholicism. "This was no small change for us!" they explained. Richard had been an atheist and Jane a fallen-away Protestant. As though that wasn't enough change in life, the couple felt God was prompting them to return to college to study art.

Richard and Jane gave up their small business, bought a small house trailer, and moved it to a small college town. When they decided to attend a larger college in another town, they planted their trailer on Bethel Island, located in the Sacramento River Delta. It was a long commute via a bridge to and from college, but the rent was cheap. Even so, money was getting tighter by the day.

The couple went to class, did their homework, and prayed fervently for God's provision. "We found ourselves scrounging around for loose change just to fill the gas tank to make it to class," they remembered, adding that gas at the time cost $1.80 per gallon. "Even the lowly pennies were precious!"

Their trust in God would be tested even more. When their Volkswagen Bug gave up the ghost, Richard and Jane were left with just their thumbs out to hitch a ride to school. But they were determined. As often happens, heaven intervened at the eleventh hour and Richard got a high-paying job that pulled them through.

Today, Richard and Jane are accomplished artists and have their trust securely placed in God. They're thankful for the quarters, dimes, nickels—yes, even the pennies—that helped them make a big change in life.

The Penny "Drops"

"My God will fully supply whatever you need," begins Philippians 4:19. For one Franciscan friar, pulling off a penny prank was a need of the humorous order.

Years ago, Brother Marian Battaglia, OFM, a Franciscan friar with the Province of St. John the Baptist in Cincinnati, was stationed at St. Clement Friary, also in Cincinnati. Whenever Brother Marian and his friar friend Brother Dominic Lococo had dinner together, Brother Marian would invariably mention his pursuit of pennies.

"It seems that every morning he would take a walk in a nearby park and find ten, fifteen, and even twenty pennies," explained Brother Dominic.

One day after Brother Marian had gone to his heavenly reward, Brother Dominic was visiting St. Clement Friary when he happened to mention Brother Marian's extraordinary penny finds to Father Curt Lanzrath, OFM. Bellows of laughter erupted as Father Curt confessed to the mischievous deed. Arising early for his morning walk, Father Curt would scatter pennies along the path Brother Marian was sure to take later.

"You might say it cost Father Curt a pretty penny," said Brother Dominic, chuckling, "but it was worth every cent to him to hear Brother Marian brag about finding all those pennies!"

"Whatsoever you sow, that you shall reap," the saying goes. Who knows? Maybe Brother Marian is having the last laugh and sowing pennies from heaven along Father Curt's path. The prankster-friar admits to finding a penny or two.

The Miracle Penny

When a family is destitute and hungry, finding a penny can be a miracle from heaven. That's the inspiring faith story of a western Pennsylvania family in the early 1940s.

"Mom and Dad were struggling to keep a roof over our heads and put food on the table for their two children," reminisced Margaret Bowser of Cleveland. "Mom was raised by a widowed Romanian immigrant who taught her how to make soup from just about anything, including all kinds of beans, especially red kidney beans. Beans expanded and filled the stomachs of many for just pennies. Red kidney beans back then cost seven cents a pound."

One day, Margaret's parents had only six cents, not enough to buy a pound of beans to quiet the growling stomachs of their hungry family. The search for the much-needed penny began—in pockets, purses, junk drawers, and down the insides of an overstuffed sofa, but to no avail.

"Desperate to find a penny for food, the search now began in desperate places," Margaret explained.

At the time, Margaret and her family were living in a large old house that had seen many families come and go. The floors were covered in much-worn linoleum, the edges chipped and torn and not tacked down. Margaret's parents went from room to room, lifting up the edges of the linoleum, begging heaven for a miracle. Finally, under a loose sheet of linoleum, they found a lone copper penny, with "In God We Trust" stamped on the front and wheat sheaves on the back.

"My mother trusted in God to provide her family with their daily bread (beans) and he did!" said Margaret, who had heard the story of the miracle penny over and over as she was growing up and how vital a penny can be in people's lives. "I would never pass up a penny anywhere! The story is forever burned in my head and my heart—and what the symbols on the penny mean to our family."

The Fret-Not Pennies

Have no worry about tomorrow, this penny tale tells us.

Several times in her life when funds were in short supply, Susan Hunt of Grants Pass, Oregon, noticed a pattern. She would look down and find a penny on the sidewalk, by the side of the road, or in a parking lot.

"Sometimes I would see two pennies a day, or find a penny three days in a row," remembered Susan. "Although these did not add up to large amounts, I felt they were a sign that I should not fret, that my needs were known, and that I was being watched over. They were truly pennies from heaven!"

Pennies for Priests

God can use the humble penny to accomplish great things. That's the testimony of praying women in the Diocese of St. Petersburg, Florida.

PENNY PRAYERS

In 2002, the St. Petersburg Diocesan Council of Catholic Women (DCCW) began a unique prayer campaign. Whenever they find a stray penny—on the ground, at the bottom of their purse, or at the grocery checkout counter—they pick it up and say a prayer for vocations to the priesthood in their diocese.

"For us, a penny saved is more than a penny earned," explained Lynn Erickson, president of the St. Petersburg DCCW. "Each penny represents a prayer from the heart for good men to answer the call and serve as priests in our diocese."

The campaign, called A Penny a Prayer for Priests, is simple. Each woman designates a jar for her pennies. When a penny is found and a prayer is said for vocations, it goes into the jar. Some women deposit their prayed pennies in a bottle decorated as a priest in a cassock, a visual reminder to "ask and you shall receive."

In 2006, the St. Petersburg DCCW began tracking the number of pennies prayed. As of April 1, 2013, an astonishing 735,596 prayers for vocations were reported—that's $7,355.96 in found pennies!

Are the penny prayers working?

"Yes!" said Lynn, adding that the found money is donated to the diocese for seminarian education. "We've seen the number of men entering the seminary grow as A Penny a Prayer for Priests became a permanent DCCW program in our diocese. The major seminary is full, and a new wing is being planned."

When prayed with faith, the humble penny is priceless!

Note: Nickels and dimes can also be prayed for religious vocations. For example, "nickels for nuns" and "dimes for deacons."

The Penny Car

If anyone needs to trust God, it's a mother and daughter buying a used car. What make and model would be best? Is the salesman honest? As Rachel Cook and her mother discovered, heaven can provide in the most unusual way.

Rachel and her widowed mother had spent several weeks in the spring of 2007 visiting numerous car dealerships around Dallas. They test drove several makes and models, but none seemed right for Rachel. And so the hunt continued. One day while they were visiting yet another dealership, the salesman said he had found a used car that fit Rachel's wants and needs at a dealership about an hour away.

"Would you wait for the dealership to drive it over?" the salesman asked them.

It was a glorious spring day, so Rachel and

her mother sat on the curb and waited, asking God for a sign about the car. About an hour later, a silver Acura pulled up next to them. As the driver got out, a penny fell out of the car and rolled over to their feet. Rachel and her mother looked at each other, astounded. It was their sign from above!

"Honey, this is your new car!" Rachel's mother exclaimed.

Rachel drove the used Acura for several years without incident, always grateful for the penny from heaven that steered them to just the right car on that memorable spring day.

Queen of the Pennies

A "penny war" for God? Yes, if it helps to meet the needs of others!

For many years, the "fight" was on at St. Elizabeth Academy, a now-closed all-girls Catholic high school in St. Louis. This was no ordinary fight, but a "holy war" to raise the most pennies for the mission field.

"The freshmen-through-senior classes each selected a candidate for Penny Queen," explained Sister Marilyn Schneider, CPPS, a 1960 graduate of the academy founded in 1882 by her Order, the Sisters of the Most Precious Blood. "Each candidate had a large glass jar in the cafeteria, and during lunchtime, students dropped pennies and spare change in their candidate's jar."

As the mountains of coins grew, so did the suspense. When the contest was over, a dance was held for the entire school. As the candidates' escorts twirled them around the dance floor, hearts were beating fast with anticipation. Finally, the announcement was made.

"The Penny Queen was the girl who had collected the most money," explained Sister Marilyn, adding that it was always a big surprise. "I remember wrapping hundreds and hundreds of pennies in coin wrappers and taking the heavy load to the bank."

And the missionaries? The money was like manna from heaven!

Note: St. Elizabeth Academy closed in 2013, but the Penny Queen tradition continues at other Catholic schools in the St. Louis area and around the country.

Penny Delight

To many people, the penny is just a useless coin. But to Deborah Ann Erdmann of Manitowoc, Wisconsin, a penny is one of God's many treasures.

Deborah was walking the shores of Lake Michigan one day when her thoughts drifted back to the carefree days of her childhood. "Whenever my little friends and I went for a walk, we always looked for coins on the ground," Deborah said. "We were seeking worldly treasures."

Walking with her head down, her eyes scanning the beach, Deborah wondered in her girlish imagination what treasures she might find in the sand that day. A gold nugget? A jagged diamond? A valuable seashell? Or perhaps a quarter?

"Suddenly, it hit me how ridiculous this was," said Deborah, author of the humorous book *The Inside Scoop on God* (www.deboraherdmann.com). "The treasure was all around me—the cinnamon-sugared sand, the white-capped waves, the seagulls sailing in the breeze—all of God's creation is a treasure!"

As Deborah surveyed the beauty of the beach, she thanked God for a world filled with treasures and then continued walking when something shiny caught her eye. "Right in front of me was a brand-new penny in the sand," said Deborah. "I'd been walking the same path up and down the beach and didn't see it before. God had added one more treasure to the beach. He loves to delight his children!"

The "Counterfeit Coin"

God is in everything—even a counterfeit coin.

One day during a pilgrimage to the Holy Land, Nettie Herrera of Guadalupita, New Mexico, was feeling a pang of sadness. She dearly missed her deceased daughter, Miranda, and needed comforting. While walking down an ancient road paved with stone, she spotted a small, round, silver-colored object. Thinking it was a shekel—an Israeli coin—Nettie picked it up, put it in her pocket, and out of habit, prayed, "In God We Trust."

"I immediately felt peace in my heart," said Nettie, a devotee of the penny prayer. Later that day she took out the shekel, not knowing if she'd be able to read or understand the coin. To Nettie's astonishment, the shekel wasn't a shekel but a cell-phone battery!

"In God We Trust"—words so powerful they can recharge a life, whether prayed with a counterfeit coin or the real thing.

An Inspiring Motto

"In God We Trust"—Four powerful words: words that lift souls to heaven. Words that call heaven down to earth. Words so majestic that when Francis Scott Key penned the lyrics for *The Star Spangled Banner*, America's national anthem, during the War of 1812, he proclaimed "In God We Trust" as the country's motto. The fourth stanza reads in part:

Blest with vict'ry and peace,
 may the heav'n rescued land
Praise the power that hath made and
 preserv'd us a nation!
Then conquer we must,
 when our cause it is just.
And this our motto, "In God is our trust."

It would take an act of Congress, however, before the words appeared on American coins. According to the U.S. Treasury, increased religious sentiment during the Civil War prompted many citizens to beseech the Treasury to declare on the nation's coins their trust in God. In a letter dated

November 13, 1861, the Reverend M. R. Watkinson of Ridleyville, Pennsylvania, petitioned Secretary of the Treasury Salmon P. Chase to recognize the "Almighty God in some form on our coins....This would place us openly under the Divine protection we have personally claimed."

Secretary Chase subsequently instructed James Pollock, director of the Mint in Philadelphia, to design a motto for the country's currency, stating, "No nation can be strong except in the strength of God, or safe except in His defense. The trust of our people in God should be declared on our national coins."

Beginning in 1864, Congress passed various laws authorizing the motto "In God We Trust" to be inscribed on American coins. The motto first appeared on the 1864 two-cent coin and has been in continuous use on the penny since 1909 and on the dime since 1916. Since 1938, all U.S. coins have borne the motto.

The Cold War during the mid-twentieth century inspired another wave of religious sentiment. On July 30, 1956, President Dwight D. Eisenhower approved a Joint Resolution of the 84th Congress and declared "In God We Trust" the national motto of the United States. The law also mandated the phrase be printed on all paper currency.

Today, every American coin and every paper bill is inscribed with four words of divine hope: "In God We Trust."

Chapter Two

Pennies of Guidance: In God We Trust for Direction in Life

God continually guides us and speaks to us. His signs are all around us. For example, a passage from a book might quicken our spirit, or a friend may unknowingly affirm a decision we're contemplating. Nature is filled with revelation. As the stories in this chapter illuminate, guidance might also come in the form of a penny.

The Penny Decision

Life is full of decisions. Which college should I attend? Is this the right person to marry? Rita Waldref of Spokane, Washington, was facing an agonizing job decision—until she found hope on a penny.

"I was discerning whether I should leave the parish where I had ministered for thirteen years," explained Rita. "I loved the parishioners and enjoyed the ministry, but a change in priests had the parish in turmoil. I spent much of my time smoothing things out, and I was depleted physically, mentally, and spiritually."

With two daughters in college, Rita wondered how she and her husband would support them if she resigned from her position. One day while anguishing over what to do, Rita stepped onto the porch of her house and saw a shiny 1998 penny.

"I was surprised to see the penny because I was certain it wasn't there when I'd entered the house earlier," she said. "I picked it up and saw the words 'In God We Trust.' I began to cry. Here was God's message: 'You can move on. I will care for you.'"

Within a month of leaving her job, Rita was offered a part-time position at another parish—a job where she could pursue her passions for liturgy and social ministry, as well as complete her master's degree in pastoral ministry.

"The penny sits proudly on the windowsill in my home office," said Rita, "a continual reminder of the trust I placed in God so many years ago."

Penny Intercession

When Elizabeth Sherrill picked up a penny, she discovered an exciting new way to pray.

"Pray!" John Sherrill told his wife, Elizabeth, as he left their New York home to fly to Grand Rapids, Michigan, for a critical business meeting the following afternoon. At 2:00 PM on September 6, 1982, John and their partner, Len LeSourd, would take part in merger talks between their small publishing company, Chosen Books, and the much larger Christian publisher Zondervan.

Before going to sleep that night, Elizabeth reached for her Bible. "Whenever I tried to pray without the aid of Scripture, my thoughts were invariably bogged down on the problems," she explained, adding there were plenty of those in the current situation.

"What about the particular kind of Christian publishing we believed God had called us to? Could it survive such a merger? What about the Chosen staff in Lincoln, Virginia? Some of them had moved families there, bought homes. Would they be uprooted? Lose their jobs?"

(The prolific authors of dozens of inspirational books—including *The Hiding Place*, *God's Smuggler*, *The Cross and the Switchblade*, as well as thousands of articles—John and

Elizabeth Sherrill and their partner, Len LeSourd, had founded Chosen Books in 1970 and dedicated it to developing new Christian writers. Chosen Book's first title was *Born Again* by Charles Colson.)

As it happened, Elizabeth also had a trip scheduled for the following day, a drive to upstate New York. It was a beautiful autumn day, and her route was a spectacular one through the Catskill Mountains. About midday Elizabeth passed an irresistible wooden signpost: "Escarpment Trail."

Elizabeth parked the car in the rest area and set out on foot up the mountainside. "The path climbed through a pine and oak forest so silent and splendid that by the time I looked at my watch it was already two o'clock, the hour I'd assured John I'd be remembering him and Len in Grand Rapids." About a hundred yards off the trail, she spotted a low outcropping of rock, worked her way to it through the tangled branches, sat down, and closed her eyes.

"But instead of intercession, what came into my mind in that whispering silence beneath the pines was a string of self-accusations. Maybe God had never wanted us to get into publishing in the first place. Or maybe he had—still did. Maybe this merger idea was only our own wishful way out of the cash-flow problems created by the past year's recession."

Elizabeth knew this kind of fretting was not prayer. But her Bible, which could have put these issues into perspective, was in the car miles away at the foot of the mountain. *How could I stop my mind from running in problem-centered circles?* she asked herself. *How could I really, meaningfully hold up the men meeting in Grand Rapids?*

Elizabeth opened her eyes—and blinked. On the ground, not two feet away, lay a bright copper penny. Elizabeth reached down and picked it up. She could not imagine how a shiny new coin came to be lying on that remote mountain slope a hundred yards from the trail. Elizabeth sat staring at it as though it were the first penny she'd ever seen.

Lincoln's profile. Arching over his head the words "In God We Trust." Below was the year "1982" and the word "Liberty."

Why, I wasn't holding just a penny! Elizabeth suddenly knew. *Here were the themes for my prayer:*

"In God We Trust"—not in our skill at negotiating. The welfare of our employees, the books we were to publish, God had the answers to these concerns! "This afternoon in Grand Rapids, Father, let Len and John take a new step in trusting you," Elizabeth began praying.

"1982." He wasn't the God of a distant past or an imaginary future; he was God of the present moment. "Father, show Len and John your will, for now, for this situation."

"Liberty." Freedom for the captives—of any and every kind—was always the will of God. "Father, release Len and John to use the skills you've given them—to work with words and not with numbers." And for those whose skills were different, those with God's gifts of business management and marketing, "Father, let the decisions in Grand Rapids mean new liberty for them as well."

God. Trust. Liberty. Elizabeth's penny prayer went on so long that she became conscious of the hard rock beneath her. Three words in Latin on the reverse side of the coin caught Elizabeth's attention as she stood up: *E pluribus unum*—"out of many, one." *Was God telling me with a chuckle that the merger was his answer,* she wondered, *that out of these two companies a single one was to emerge?*

That was, as it turned out, the result of the deliberations that afternoon in Grand Rapids. The merger of Zondervan and Chosen Books permitted the Sherrills and Len LeSourd to keep their staff in Lincoln and pursue their particular philosophy of publishing.[*]

"I didn't know this as I hiked down the mountain that September afternoon with a penny in my pocket," Elizabeth says. "I only knew I had a secret to intercession anywhere I found myself. God has filled the world with clues to his presence; the humblest object can remind us that God is in charge."

In 1992, Chosen Books was sold to Baker Books Publishing Group.

Adapted and reprinted with permission from the book When God Breaks Through *by John and Elizabeth Sherrill.*

"CENT-imental" Cents

A penny is a penny, right? Not if you're Tim Renzelmann of Sheboygan, Wisconsin. When Tim was hospitalized for cancer, a fifty-dollar bag of pennies not only turned his fear to joy but transformed his life. This is Tim's amazing journey of the CENT-imental cents.

Tim, who is undoubtedly the master of the penny pun, began collecting pennies at age eight while helping his brother, Terry, with a paper route. "As I grew into adulthood, I would often turn to pennies during stressful periods of my life," Tim explained. "Sorting through the pennies in search of the occasional wheat cent, the rare Indian cent, or other collectibles provided me a 'CENTS' of calm and tranquility."

On May 11, 1992, at the age of twenty-nine, Tim was diagnosed with cancer. To deal with the stress, Tim began making routine trips to the bank where Terry worked to pick up more pennies. After five months of chemotherapy and radiation treatments, Tim's cancer went into remission. Four years later the cancer returned. Though Tim underwent more aggressive treatment, the cancer continued to spread.

"By mid-1998, the cancer had invaded my chest, abdomen, pelvis, and bone marrow," explained Tim. "My best hope for long-term remission would be an allogeneic bone-marrow transplant. As it turned out, Terry was a perfect match and provided the 'e-CENT-ial' life-saving bone marrow that I needed."

Tim spent many nights in the hospital before the scheduled transplant. One Friday, Terry stopped by and plopped down a fifty-dollar bag of pennies (that's 5,000 pennies!) at the foot of Tim's bed. "I thought you might want these," he told Tim.

Eventually, Tim's wife, parents, and brother went home, and Tim was left hooked up to IVs and feeling miserable and lonely. Tim pulled the bag onto his lap, cracked open the first roll of pennies, and one by one began examining each coin.

"I'm not sure why, but I started playing a game of 'reminis-CENTS,'" said Tim. "As I examined each coin, I looked at the date and then thought back to that year of my life and recalled a good thought—a pleasant experience, a fond memory, a special friend, a considerate gift, a kind gesture, a memorable event, or anything else I could think of. At first it was easy, but every time the year on a penny repeated itself, I was forced to look back at my life with greater detail and clarity."

Tim found himself thinking about things he hadn't thought about in years. He thought about his childhood years, his high school years, and his college years. Tim thought about his first job of delivering newspapers and the many other jobs that followed. He thought about loving family members, good friends, and many wonderful acquaintances.

"I thought about the many experiences of life that brought me to where I was at that very moment," continued Tim. "Each penny represented a 'CENT-sational' person, a 'magnifi-CENT' memory, or one of the many other gifts that this life had bestowed on me. Before long, my sorrow turned to joy, my anger succumbed to appreciation, my fears yielded to gratitude, and my despair was replaced with hope!"

As the night ended, Tim collected one penny from each year from his birth to the then-current year of 1998. When he got home, he placed them in a small velvet bag. "These coins became known as my CENT-imental cents, and I carried them with me just about everywhere I went. The next time I found myself waiting anxiously in the doctor's office for the next batch of results, whenever sorrow, anger, fear, or despair came my way, I pulled out my CENT-imental cents and played the game again."

Many years have passed since Tim's bone-marrow transplant, and he remains in remission. "Over the years, this humble little coin has helped me to develop a 'common cents' approach to cancer," said Tim, now a patient advocate and cancer coach at a Sheboygan clinic. "The penny has taught me to make CENTS of life's challenges, it has reminded me to 'ac-CENT-tuate' the positives, and it 'repre-CENTS' what is truly valuable in life."

In gratitude for his health and his life, Tim wrote the following prayer:

My Penny Prayer
O, Magnifi-CENT One!
You are at the CENT-er of all that is good!
We give you thanks for this CENT-sational
  day
And for the love and com-PENNY

*Of those you have CENT into our lives,
As together we search for a greater CENTS of
   hope
As we read the words, "In God We Trust."*

Penny Reassurance

There are many "whys" in life. Why this or why that? In 2002, Linda Rose of Fairfield, Ohio, had a penny experience that was full of whys.

After a visit with Linda's brother in Fresno, California, Linda, her husband, and their son were preparing for the long drive back to Ohio. They said their goodbyes at 6:00 AM and stopped at a nearby convenience store for orange juice. As the guys went into the store, Linda decided to stretch her legs. She knew she'd be sitting a spell before their next rest break. As people often do, Linda worried about the trip ahead of them: their safety, the road conditions, that nothing would go wrong with the car.

"Walking around the car I found three pennies on the ground," said Linda, adding that an overwhelming sense of calmness enveloped her as she picked them up. "I could almost hear God saying, 'Calm down, worrywart: I'll get you home safe and sound.'"

And he did.

But Linda wondered about the "whys" of

that morning. Why did they stop at that particular store? Why did she get out after being in the car for just a few minutes? Why was she looking down when she was only walking around the car? Why were there pennies on the ground at that particular parking spot? And, most important, why were there three pennies?

"Because there were three of us," said Linda, certain the pennies were heaven-sent to reassure them of divine protection as they began the 2,300-mile stretch of interstate back to Ohio. Their journey was so peaceful, in fact, that they might have been traveling "heaven's highway," their car filled with angels along for the ride.

The Penny Prayer Walk

When Karen Davis of Grand Junction, Colorado, found four pennies during a prayer walk one day, she discovered a healing lesson.

On July 11, 2006, Karen was out walking and praying, something she does every day. It was a particularly hard season in Karen's life. She had recently resigned her pastoral position at her church, which wasn't easy for her to do, and she was suffering from tremendous physical pain. Doctor after doctor had examined Karen, but none offered a definitive diagnosis. The source of the pain remained a mystery.

PENNY PRAYERS

"Something was terribly wrong with my body," said Karen. "My entire left side felt like it was on fire, and my body was clearly fighting off some sort of infection, but was it? I was losing weight and losing my balance. My vision was changing. I couldn't sleep. My blood pressure was dropping, and my lymph nodes were the size of golf balls. I didn't know what to do or where to turn."

During Karen's prayer walk that morning, a friend called her cell phone and said he'd unexpectedly lost his job. Karen stopped walking, sat down on the sidewalk, and began to pray with him. As she leaned back, she put her hand in a pile of pennies. When their conversation was over, Karen picked up the pennies and continued walking.

"As I was rolling the four pennies around in my hand, I felt God was trying to say something to me," explained Karen, a youth-ministry leader and mother of two teenagers. "I asked him, 'What is the message?' Quickly, it came to me: *Believe 4* (there were four pennies) *my provision. Trust me.*"

Intrigued by the penny find, Karen researched the history of the penny and discovered "In God We Trust" has appeared on the Lincoln penny since 1909. What happened next is truly "*cent*-sational." Since that July morning,

Karen has found at least one penny or coin every day—22,314 coins as of May 15, 2013!

"When the pennies kept coming, I realized God was telling me to make the needed changes in life and to trust him," said Karen, adding that her recovery began when she recognized body and spirit are interconnected and then asked herself some tough questions: What was making my spirit sick? What was suppressing my health and vitality to the point my body couldn't fight off a common virus? What emotional burden is my body carrying?

"This process was filled with many painful discoveries and forced me to admit things I didn't want to admit because the emotional pain would be as great as the physical pain," said Karen, an organizational consultant who mentors pastors and leaders of faith-based organizations. "For months I felt as though I was hanging upside down by my heels so everything that needed to go from my life would shake out. 'Trust me with the change,' God seemed to whisper in my ear every time I found a penny."

Several months later Karen's symptoms were in remission, and she continues to enjoy good health. In 2007, she launched www.cantsparethechange.com and began blogging about her penny finds and the messages they seem to hold.

"I never find pennies behind me," explained Karen. "They're always ahead of me or next to me, which is the same with God. He's present in my today and already inhabits my tomorrow. One penny and one day at a time, God has proven his trustworthiness to me. I can fear not!"

The Penny Proposal

Where can a trail of pennies lead? To a life of joy and happiness!

"I knew from the start that Jesse and I had something special," said Hui R. of Fullerton, California, whose last name is withheld. "However, when I began dating Jesse, my parents forbade it due to our cultural differences. Whenever I asked for divine guidance on how to keep my budding relationship with Jesse and my relationship with my parents, I found pennies."

The pennies seemed to be telling Hui to trust and all would be well. Yet Hui was in deep turmoil; she wanted to honor her parents, but she loved Jesse. She didn't know what to do or where to turn. Pennies kept coming her way.

One day more than a year and a half into their blossoming relationship, the couple headed to their usual hiking spot. Hui spotted a penny by a cluster of tall, silvery-leafed bushes off to the side of the trail. Then she spied another penny and another. Around the bushes Hui went, merrily collecting the pennies. Suddenly she realized what was happening.

"Excited and nervous, I called out to Jesse from behind the bushes," Hui laughed. "The trail of pennies rounded the bushes and led to a white ring box with a penny on top. Jesse was sitting nearby, grinning mischievously. Needless to say, my answer was yes!"

After an extended engagement, the couple was married. Hui's parents grew to appreciate and love Jesse—and their first grandson. Just as the pennies seemed to predict, Hui trusted and all is well.

Penny, Thou Art Loosed!

Sometimes even the smallest things can guide us to the deeper things of God. That's the message of this humorous account of a "sticky penny."

"Rats. I had forgotten to bring my secret offering. As the Communion music ended, I opened my purse to find nothing but a wheat-back penny," reminisced Jeanette Levellie, a pastor's wife in Paris, Illinois, and a prolific writer and speaker. Jeanette had a fondness for wheat backs and had collected them for years.

(From 1909 to 1958, the Lincoln penny featured on the "tails" side two sheaves of wheat flanking the words "one cent" and "United States of America." The coin is commonly called a "wheat penny" or "wheat back.")

"It's not that I begrudge you this wheat back, Lord," Jeanette said silently, "but what about the deacon who sees me put it in the plate? He might go home and tell his wife how I put only a penny in the offering. They'd shake their heads at my stingy attitude. Since I'm the preacher's wife, I should maintain a little dignity here, don't you think, Lord?"

No answer.

Several months earlier, the Lord had nudged Jeanette to give an offering whenever she attended church. He didn't require a set amount. He only asked that she bring something in addition to her tithe every time she came to church.

Jeanette thought perhaps the Lord was trying to teach her to show more appreciation for him in a tangible way. Or that giving more would increase her love for his people. *Yes, that must be it,* Jeanette mused. *I generally love Jesus and his church; it's people who challenge my resolve to walk in love.*

During the first few weeks Jeanette obeyed with ease and didn't tell anyone except her husband about her secret offerings. But soon "my obedience grew horns of smugness," Jeanette said. "Not only was I giving extra each week, I was giving in secret. Wow. I impressed myself with my devotion to the Lord."

Until this Sunday.

"Lord, I'm the minister's wife," Jeanette wailed in her heart. "Won't I set a poor example putting a penny in the plate?"

Still no answer.

Then Jeanette remembered the admonition in 1 Samuel 15:22: "Obedience is better than sacrifice." "The Lord was asking me to toss down my pride by giving him a penny—one cent," she said. "The wheat back was worth, at most, five cents to a coin dealer. Much more to him who saw my secret motives."

Jeanette slipped the penny onto the crimson felt plate and bowed her head, pretending to appear nonchalant.

"I'd love to tell you that since that day, strangers have flagged me down on the street to put hundred-dollar bills in my hand or that someone anonymously paid off our car loan," Jeanette laughed.

Instead, she received a greater blessing: a corner of her heart was set free. "I've always longed to obey the Lord, to do whatever he told me, without question, without argument," she explained, "but I had a chain around my soul. I worried what people thought of me, especially the people in our church. I cared too much for their respect and not enough for God's applause.

"If I ever become wealthy and the Lord asks me to give it all away," continued Jeanette, "I trust I will obey without a blink. It's only money, after all—not worth a cent compared to the offering of an obedient heart."

Adapted and reprinted with permission from the book Two Scoops of Grace With Chuckles on Top *by Jeanette Levellie (www.jeanettelevellie.com).*

The Penny Palace

Impossible to possible! That's the incredible but true story of the Penny Palace and the power of the motto, "In God We Trust."

For thirty years, Doc and Tina Shelton of Pomona, California, had a dream: to build a house on an acre of rural land that Doc had acquired long before their dating days. As often happens in life, things did not go according to plan.

"When we got married, our first home was a fixer-upper close to Doc's job as an engineering professor at Cal Poly Pomona and where I was a student," explained Tina. "We expected to live there three to five years before moving on."

The years turned into decades. There were jobs, the kids and their education, plus numer-

PENNY PRAYERS

ous volunteer and community involvements. Finally, when the kids were grown with homes of their own, Doc and Tina rekindled their dream and hired an architect. Then one night they arrived home to discover a burst water line had flooded their house. They put their construction plans on hold and instead focused on major repair work.

Eventually, construction plans were back on the table, and the process began again. This time an unexpected family situation arose, and all thoughts of building were abandoned for the next two years.

Doc was nearing retirement, and the couple was hoping to celebrate their twenty-fifth wedding anniversary in their dream home, so efforts began a third time. After many months of working with the city, their housing plans were approved. Everything looked green—for go!

Then Tina went to obtain the first permit. "The city was going to require sidewalks, a handicap ramp, street lighting, irrigation, street widening and more to the public areas before allowing the house to be built," said Tina. "Those public improvements would cost more than half of our working budget!"

Months of negotiation with the city led to no resolution. Thus, Doc and Tina's dream home was abandoned a third time. While the couple was grieving their loss, the housing market took a free-fall and few banks were offering construction loans. Yet strangely, Tina felt a "nudge" to build.

"I had no reasonable explanation for wanting to build," remembered Tina, adding that she dubbed her dream house "Tina's Ark." Like Noah, who built an ark with no rain clouds in sight, Tina also was building in faith—and being tested mightily along the way.

One day in December 2008, Tina cried out in desperation, "Look here, Powers that be! This is a foolish and costly endeavor. If you want me to build this ark, then you'd better show me a sign—maybe a penny or something—if I am to proceed."

The next day a penny appeared. And the next day. And the next day. And the day after that. After ten consecutive days, Tina figured she had a fairly strong "yes" to proceed.

"It was shocking to reach 100 consecutive days of finding pennies and then 200 days," reminisced Tina, an engineering educator at Cal Poly Pomona. "There were forces at work that defied any earthly explanations. What is the mathematical probability of such a 'winning' streak?"

Tina started a blog about her penny finds (www.pennyfinders.com) and called the beings that dropped pennies in her path the "penny angels." In August of 2009, Tina told them, "Finding pennies for 225 days is nice, but don't you think stronger actions are needed if you expect me to build this ark?"

Two days later, Doc and Tina's son called them about a parcel of land in foreclosure that was located in a beautiful area where he dreamed of living. Tina laughingly said, "Just the bare land there would cost almost our entire construction budget. That area is too ritzy for common folk like us. Impossible!"

Even so, over the next several days, Doc and Tina evaluated the situation and the property. The following Monday, they went to the city offices to determine the necessary public works, permits, and approximate fees. That afternoon they made an offer to the bank, and the following day it was accepted.

Doc and Tina proceeded to design an entirely new set of house plans and over the next year to obtain the necessary authorizations from various city agencies. On his official report, the soils engineer called the project the "Penny Palace"—and the name stuck. Finally, on Valentine's Day 2011 (day 787 of penny finds), construction began.

During the fifteen months of construction, Tina continued to find at least one coin every day. "They served as reminders to trust and to take it one day at a time," explained Tina. "There was one story after another of COIN-cidences (also known as miracles) when impossible situations somehow became possible."

The house was becoming much more than concrete and lumber. Amazingly, the subcontractors and their families, coworkers, neighbors, and others also began finding pennies and seeing possibilities in their own lives.

"Sometimes the answer we're looking for may be lying there unnoticed, just like a penny on the ground," commented Tina. "We need to release all worries about how we'll achieve things and be receptive for the answers to reveal themselves."

In May 2012, Doc and Tina moved into their "palace." That October, they hosted an open house, with hundreds of friends, students, coworkers, subcontractors, family members, and penny-tale readers converging to celebrate the palace and the inspirational power of a penny. During the festivities, which lasted several days, Tina did not leave the palace and, thus, her consecutive string of penny finding ended—on Day 1,393: three years and ten months of daily finds!

Impossible?

The Penny Palace is a symbol of the "possible."

Making "Cents" of Illness

When Nancy Roberts of Woodbury, Minnesota, learned in 2002 she had an irreversible disease, she feared the future. But a penny changed her perspective—and her life.

Nancy and her husband were sitting on a bench in a shopping center waiting for her doctor's appointment. Ten weeks earlier, Nancy had been diagnosed with multiple sclerosis (MS) that, in Nancy's case, primarily affected her vision.

"I had to take a leave of absence from my job as a registered nurse in a hospital operating room," explained Nancy, "and I was hoping for medical clearance to return to my job."

As Nancy and her husband waited, their minds were bombarded with thoughts about the future. *What is going to happen to our finances if Nancy can't work? What if Nancy can no longer drive? What if Nancy's MS keeps getting worse and she ends up in a wheelchair? What if Nancy's vision continues to darken?* Their list of fears grew with each passing moment.

Then Nancy looked down at the floor, her eyes spilling with tears, and spotted a lone penny.

"It was heads up," said Nancy. "As I bent over to pick up the penny, I noticed Abe Lincoln's head had spots on it, probably from all the fingers that had touched it. I smiled as I thought, *Hey, Abe's got MS, too!*" (MS causes spots on your brain that show up on MRI scans.)

But it was the words engraved above Honest Abe's head that jumped out at Nancy. "In God We Trust," they said. *That's it!* Nancy thought, her heart exploding with faith. *We need to trust.*

Nancy was able to return to work, and she admits that she's a better nurse and a more understanding person because of her health issue. "What I learned from that penny is invaluable," Nancy said, who began writing and in 2009 published *Heaven Cent Prayers*, a book that exhorts readers to put their unique situations in the Lord's hands and trust him.

"Watching the Lord take the situations in our lives, work in them, and make 'cents' of them is amazing," Nancy said. "How that penny got under that bench in that particular shopping center, at that time, on that day, I don't know. It was a God thing."

The Penny Trust

What to do with all those found pennies? Start a "trust fund," says Sister Charlene Diorka, SSJ.

"The call to live the religious life is a journey of trust—a call that will be tested many times," explained Sister Charlene, formation director for the Sisters of St. Joseph in Philadelphia, recalling one particular test that became a life lesson.

Sister Charlene had been struggling with a ministry situation and found it difficult to pray. "I wondered where God was, and why God couldn't make things better," she said, adding that her restlessness led her to take morning walks in the neighborhood. "One morning I saw a penny. I picked it up and pocketed it."

Later that day, Sister Charlene was closing down her computer when she noticed a forwarded e-mail from an acquaintance. She usually deleted those frequently forwarded e-mails, but this time the subject line caught her attention.

"Pennies!" it read.

"I hurriedly opened the e-mail and read an incredible story that seemed like God's answer to my prayer," continued Sister Charlene. "One part really touched my heart":

Whenever I find a coin I see the inscription, "In God We Trust." It is written on every single United States coin, but we never seem to notice it! God drops a message right in front of us, telling us to trust him! Who am I to pass it by? When I see a coin, I pray. I stop to see if my trust IS in God at that moment. I pick up the coin as a response to God that I do trust in him. For a short time, at least, I cherish it as if it were gold. I think it's God's way of starting a conversation with me. Lucky for me, God is patient, and pennies are plentiful!

Since then, Sister Charlene began finding pennies on a more frequent basis. "I saved every one and began my 'trust fund,'" she said. "The ministry situation became more difficult, yet my trust in God deepened. No matter what happened, I became keenly aware that God is always with me and I am called to trust. God is patient, and I know firsthand that pennies are plentiful!"

Penny Perspectives

Life is full of options. Do I do this or that? Which invitations get a "yes" or a "no"? Sometimes we have so many options that we opt out and become a hermit instead. That was the case for Leslie Stein until she discovered "penny perspectives."

On December 29, 2006, Leslie found a twenty-dollar bill in the crosswalk on her way home from work in Washington, D.C. She picked it up, did a happy dance, and treated herself to a pedicure. As she was getting her toes done, Leslie began thinking about lost money.

How much money could I find in one year if I picked up all the coins I usually pass by? Leslie wondered. On January 1, 2007, she set out to answer that question.

PENNY PRAYERS

For one year, Leslie picked up every coin she could find: pennies on the ground by parking meters; pennies in grimy gutters; money dropped in grocery checkout lanes or in buses. There was an occasional quarter and some paper money as well. Leslie's grand total for the year was $32.76.

"The real value wasn't in the money itself," reflected Leslie. "It's what I learned from doing the project. I call them Penny Perspectives. I kept noticing things in life that I had somehow managed to forget, such as what you focus on, you find more of."

Leslie realized she had been saying "yes" to everything in life and in so doing was saying "no" to her true desires and dreams. Leslie decided to find a new project to focus on—something that could bring real change to the world, not just picking up someone's lost pocket change.

Or so she thought.

But when Leslie tried to end her penny project, fellow penny finders protested. During her one-year experiment, thirty-seven people had joined Leslie in picking up money and had amassed $44.04 on their own. Leslie was baffled by the "penny fellowship," but she went with the flow and continued the project for another year. During year two, more people joined the penny chase and more than tripled the money found in year one.

"Everywhere I went, I found pennies, even in places where it doesn't make sense for a penny to be," said Leslie. "Of course, I made it my business to look—luck favors those who take action! But there was one place I never found a penny. Nada. Zero. Zip. I never found one sitting at home like a hermit on my couch."

Six years later, pennies are still the *center*piece of Leslie's life. Taking the penny lessons that she learned, Leslie made a big change in life. She relocated to Las Vegas and now travels the globe as a speaker and life coach (www.lesliestein.com). She also wrote and published *Penny Perspectives: Let Go of Happily Ever After & Invest in Happily Ever Now.*

"My two cents' worth?" continued Leslie. "Find your passion and enjoy life!"

"What are your two cents?" she asked, offering these thought-provoking, life-changing questions:

What is the dream or desire you most want to pursue?

What things do you need to say "no" to so you can leave room for your dreams and desires?

What action can you take today that will move you one step closer to your dreams?

The Penny Confession

"Kids say the darnedest things," Art Linkletter used to say. If only he had heard young Frank Meagher's "penny confession"!

When Monsignor Meagher of Columbus, Ohio, was ordained a priest on August 6, 1960, his second-grade teacher, Mrs. Gray, was waiting in the reception line. When Mrs. Gray's turn arrived to congratulate him, she recalled a classroom incident in which she learned of Frank's aspirations to become a priest.

As the story goes, when some pennies went missing from Mrs. Gray's desk drawer, she took each student individually into the hall and asked if he or she had taken the money. When Mrs. Gray asked young Frank about the coins, he blurted out, "I didn't take them because I'm going to be a priest, and priests don't steal!"

Chapter Three

Pennies From Heaven: In God We Trust for Deceased Loved Ones

Some bereaved report seeing butterflies, the Christian symbol of new life, after a loved one dies. Others find pennies—pennies from heaven, they call them. If the "big saints," such as Thérèse of Lisieux, who often leaves roses as her calling card, can make earthly visits, why not the "little saints," our departed loved ones? As the stories in this chapter suggest, everything is possible with God, even penny visits from heaven.

Angel Pennies

A penny can console a grieving heart, this heart-warming story tells us.

When a mother becomes ill or needs to work to help support the family, oldest sisters sometimes become "junior moms." Donna Ronio of Lawton, Oklahoma, took on that role when her mother worked to support her six children. "All my life I have felt like the guardian of the family," said Donna, "the one who fixes things for the people I love." Thus, it was natural that after the family grew up, Donna still felt that way.

In 2001, Donna read several internet inspirational messages regarding pennies. "They were supposed to be little signs from heaven," she said. "I started becoming more aware of them, even looking for them." On several occasions, especially when she needed some reassurance, Donna came upon a penny lying in a parking lot or on a step. She always picked them up. Somehow they seemed more than good-luck charms.

Then Donna's younger sister, Kathy, became seriously ill with a painful form of cancer. It slowly depleted her energy until she was finally bedridden and unable to move. "On our last visit I told her that I loved her and would be back the following weekend," Donna remembered. "But she passed away before that happened."

Donna was consumed with grief, but also with guilt. Wasn't she the Big Sister who could fix anything? Had she let her sister down?

The memorial service was beautiful. Afterward, as everyone came out of the church, Donna stopped to talk to a friend of Kathy's.

"As I turned to walk away, there on the ground just in front of the toe of my shoe was a bright, shiny new 2001 penny," Donna said, "the first 2001 penny I had seen, all fresh and shiny." Just like Kathy, she realized. Relief flooded her spirit. Somehow she knew Kathy was safe and sound with Jesus, and he had sent a message to let Donna know.

"Since that day, I have found more 'angel pennies,' but none with the significance of that one, sent to ease my pain," she continued. Donna misses Kathy, but she knows they will be reunited some day.

Reprinted with permission from Joan Wester Anderson (www.joanwanderson.com).

Pennies of Everlasting Love

"Every time it rains, it rains pennies from heaven," begins the delightful tune from the 1930s. "Don't you know each cloud contains pennies from heaven?"

For many years, "pennies from heaven" was just that for Jean Cook of Garland, Texas: a cute song or dance routine her daughter's dance class performed as a recital. One day, that all changed.

Jean's husband, Kelly, passed away in September 2005, at the age of 58. "Even though I knew he wasn't well, I didn't see it coming," Jean said. Despite her loss, Jean resumed her normal activities, even returning to Mexico where she and Kelly had spent a few weeks each winter relaxing in the quaint fishing village of Bucerias, north of Puerto Vallarta.

"We always invited friends to come join us," Jean said. "Our daughters, Juli and Rachel, spent several of their winter breaks hanging out at the beach. It was a wonderful place filled with wonderful memories."

When Jean began planning her trip to Bucerias without Kelly at her side, she asked Kelly's friend Jim and his wife, Pat, to join her. Jim had been one of Kelly's closest friends and a pillar of support for Jean during Kelly's hospital stay. The balmy days and nights passed quickly, and soon it was time for Jean to drive Jim and Pat to the airport to catch their flight back to Texas.

When Jean returned to the small condo resort—her Mexican home away from home—she noticed a penny in the middle of the king-size bed in the room her guests had just vacated.

How strange, Jean thought. *Where did that come from? The maid has already changed the sheets and cleaned the room. Why would a penny be in the middle of the bed?*

While Jean speculated about the penny,

she kept her thoughts to herself. People might think that, in the throes of grief, she was imagining things.

The next day daughter Juli and family arrived in Bucerias for a getaway. Juli confided in Jean that she was having a difficult time coping with the loss of her father and caring for her new baby, Jane, born just thirteen days after he passed away. Then Juli told Jean an intriguing story.

One day back home in Colorado, Juli bundled up Jane and they set off to get a fried peach pie, one of her dad's favorites. As Juli sat relishing every bite and missing her dad, she glanced down and saw a penny near Jane's baby seat.

"It had not been there before," Juli insisted. "It's almost as though Dad left it there for me so I would know he was watching over me and the baby."

"A penny," Jean mused, again.

When Jean returned home following her winter break in Mexico, daughter Rachel met her at the airport. Around Rachel's neck was a gold chain with a penny. "Where did you get that?" Jean asked, the hair on her neck beginning to curl.

At the time, Rachel had been working as a cocktail waitress. The night before, Rachel explained, a woman was sitting alone at the bar. Draped around her neck was a penny necklace.

Rachel commented on the necklace and then went to get the woman's order. When Rachel returned, the woman took the necklace off, placed it around Rachel's neck and told her she needed to have it.

A few minutes later, Rachel went to check on her customer and—poof!—she was gone—vanished, like an angel.

Three pennies: one for Jean, one for Juli, and one for Rachel. Pennies from heaven? Signs Kelly was with them? Jean and her daughters think so. Like the round penny—without a beginning or an end—love is for eternity, in heaven and on earth.

The Penny Memorial

A penny may not be worth much financially, but it holds valuable lessons about life, especially for those grieving the loss of a loved one.

In May 1998, LeeAnn Luker and her husband of Seattle were walking across a chapel parking lot to attend the funeral service of her mother-in-law when something caught her eye: a penny. LeeAnn picked up the small copper coin and tears filled her eyes. Engraved on the front of the coin was the profile of Abraham Lincoln and the inscriptions "In God We Trust" and "Liberty."

"These words comforted me," said LeeAnn. "Yes, I *could* trust God. My mother-in-law would live again because God has promised us the hope of the resurrection. I could also trust that God would be with my father-in-law and comfort him, as well as my husband, his brother, and sisters."

There was also a message of hope in the word "Liberty," continued LeeAnn. "My mother-in-law was now liberated from the sorrows, pain, and suffering of the flesh. There was liberty for me in that understanding. I didn't have to worry about her fate or her future. I could stand fast in the liberty that 'Christ set us free'" (Galatians 5:1).

As LeeAnn walked into the chapel, she glanced at the coin and was drawn to Lincoln's profile. *Lincoln didn't just talk about his convictions but lived by them and died for them,* LeeAnn thought, as she reflected on her mother-in-law's life. She, too, had lived by her convictions. She was an honorable woman who loved God and loved her family. She lived and died holding fast to those values. And like Lincoln, she had come from humble roots. She had been born on a farm in northern Tennessee, and that simplicity had remained with her all her life.

Turning the penny over, LeeAnn was momentarily surprised. "I had forgotten that the back of the coin was engraved with the Lincoln Memorial in Washington, D.C.," LeeAnn explained. "A memorial—how fitting that seemed! Many people were filling the chapel to honor and remember my mother-in-law. But there would be no large memorial erected for her, just a simple grave marker. The biggest memorial to her would be her family—her children, grandchildren, and great-grandchildren. Her love had influenced all of their lives."

As LeeAnn continued to study the coin, she saw the Latin words *E Pluribus Unum* just above the engraving of the Lincoln Memorial. Though it had been many years since LeeAnn had studied Latin, she knew their meaning: "From many, one."

"Here, in this little sunlit chapel, people were gathering for my mother-in-law's funeral service. *Many* different religions were represented," said LeeAnn. "As I looked around, those Latin words seemed very significant. Ultimately, through the plan of God, we will all be united into one family, the family of God. The power of God will take *many* and make them *one!*"

LeeAnn turned the penny over again and noticed the coin had been minted in 1986. In the twelve years it had been in circulation, the coin had become dull with age, the engraving worn in places. But the value of the coin was not diminished by age. It was still worth one cent. With cleaning and polishing, it could even look new!

"My mother-in-law was eighty-two years old when she died," LeeAnn said. "Like the penny, she'd been around a while. She was also 'worn' by life. Her hair was gray and her face wrinkled, but just as the penny could be restored, I knew God was going to restore her. She was going to be raised incorruptible, immortal—shiny and new!

"To some, she may not have seemed all that 'valuable' either. She wasn't famous. She wasn't rich. She wasn't brilliant. She was just a simple, humble woman, like this one-cent coin. Yet she was very valuable to God."

LeeAnn slipped the "memorial penny" into her pocket, thankful for the messages of comfort it had given her—and for the godly and honorable life of her mother-in-law.

Adapted and reprinted with permission from United Church of God, www.ucg.org/christian-living/lessons-penny.

Pennies of Healing

When Nettie Herrera taught her young daughter Miranda Serna the penny prayer, she never dreamed that one day the prayer would bring healing to her own soul.

"I once told Miranda that whenever she saw a coin on the ground, she should pick it up and read 'In God We Trust' because perhaps she needed God at that very moment," said Nettie, a grandmother of three from Guadalupita, New Mexico.

Miranda not only picked up pennies, she racked up points on the basketball scoreboard. The hoops star helped the Lady Eagles at Eldorado High School in Albuquerque, New Mexico, win two consecutive state championships, and later the Lady Cardinals at Trinity Valley Community College in Athens, Texas, earn two national junior-college championships—one as a player and the other as an assistant coach.

After graduating from college, Miranda worked as an assistant women's basketball coach/recruiter at several NCAA colleges before accepting a position as lead recruiter and assistant basketball coach for the Cowgirls at Oklahoma State University (OSU) in Stillwater. Known as one of the country's best recruiters, Miranda was both charismatic and a Christian role model.

"Since she was little, Miranda had attended Mass every Sunday and on Holy Days of Obligation," said Nettie, adding that Miranda often wore a cross necklace and packed her Bible on recruiting trips. "Her job motto was 'God, Family, Education, Basketball'—in that order. She treated her players and recruits like daughters and always made me feel like a celebrity when she proudly introduced me to her basketball friends as her mom."

On November 17, 2011, Nettie's life—and the lives of countless others—was changed forever. Miranda, single and thirty-six years old, was in a fatal plane crash in central Arkansas, along with Cowgirls' head coach Kurt Budke and two OSU donors. They were en route to visit recruits at a basketball tournament.

Shortly after Miranda was laid to rest in Guadalupita, Nettie, her other daughter Cassandra, and her three children made the eight-hour drive to Stillwater. For more than a month, they stayed in Miranda's home, reminiscing and remembering the extraordinary love they had for one another.

"We would always say the three of us [Nettie, Miranda, and Cassandra] were a complete package and that some day we'd build our own 'Golden Girls' home," said Nettie. "We were always together—whether in person or by phone—and were very close to one another."

Then a mysteriously wonderful thing began to happen. "Whenever I would start feeling emotionally weak or overcome with sadness, I would find a holy medal or a coin," explained Nettie. "Sometimes I would find three pennies a day—they were in every corner of her house! I would read 'In God We Trust' and immediately find comfort and peace."

On Christmas Day, Nettie was surprised to find an angel ornament and dozens of pennies scattered around the exterior entrance of Miranda's home. How they got there, she doesn't know, but Christmas suddenly seemed more joyful.

Though years have passed since Miranda's passing, Nettie still finds pennies at precisely the moment she needs comforting. "I thank God for lending Miranda to me for thirty-six years in this life," she continued, adding that Miranda is very much alive in spirit. "I feel her presence around me, even in the pennies I find."

Nettie's penny lesson to Miranda so many years ago has returned to her, a soothing balm to her spirit and a lifter of her soul to heaven and the God in whom she trusts.

The Wedding Penny

Whenever you find a penny, pick it up because it's a message from heaven, the late Abigail Van Buren wrote years ago in her advice column, "Dear Abby."

Ever since Marie Wolfstirn of Toms River, New Jersey, read those words, she's picked up pennies. One day something wonderful happened.

"My oldest granddaughter was an only grandchild for three years," Marie explained. "My husband and I spent a great deal of time with her and grew very close to her."

Marie's husband passed away in 1998. During her granddaughter's wedding reception six years later, Marie was seated at a table near the dance floor. "I was able to watch the dancers and enjoy them and the music," she reminisced.

At the end of one dance set, after everyone had left the dance floor, Marie looked down and saw a penny on the floor in front of her. Astonished, Marie picked it up.

"I felt it was a message from my husband in heaven letting me know he was with us," said Marie. "I can think of no other explanation as to how that penny got there."

Marie still has that "wedding penny" and remembers the joy it brought her. Marie and her husband joined together in love—a love that lasts for all eternity.

Debe's Penny

The veil between this world and the next is thin—so thin the purest of heart can sometimes see a de-

ceased loved one. That's the extraordinary story of "Debe's penny."

Jane Redner was born shortly after her Grandpa Kelly passed away. When Juli, Jane's mother, began telling her stories about Grandpa, Jane, in her two-year-old talk, called him "Debe." "Debe, Debe!" she'd exclaim when she saw photos of him.

One day when Grandma Jeannie was visiting the Redner family at their Colorado home, Jane, her curly blond hair flying, dashed into the house. "Look!" she said, opening her small hand for all to see. "A penny!"

"Where did you get that?" Grandma Jeannie asked.

"Debe gave it to me," replied Jane, her blue eyes shining brightly as though she had just seen an angel.

Amazingly, that wasn't Jane's only encounter with Debe. On another occasion, Juli was pushing Jane on her swing high to the moon when Jane began telling a curious story. "Debe used to push you on the swing when you were little," said Jane, nonchalantly. "When you would swing forward, he'd pop M&M's into your mouth."

The hair on Juli's arms stood straight out like porcupine quills. "Where did you hear that story?" she asked, a bit startled. If she hadn't thought about that in years, how could Jane possibly know?

"Debe told it to me," replied Jane, with the innocence of a young child. "He comes to visit me when I'm swinging, and we laugh and talk."

Jane talked about seeing Debe for several years. Then one day Debe stopped coming. It seems that when a child reaches the age of reason, the angels or deceased loved ones they once saw become invisible. They, like their parents, must now walk in faith. But for a brief season, Jane lived in two worlds—and she has a penny to prove it.

Pennies of Passion

Sometimes pennies from heaven can help inspire a new passion in life. That's the heartfelt story of a mother and her young son, Caleb.

Caleb was two years old in early 2007 when he developed a double ear infection that would not go away, said Nichole Granville of Hawley, Pennsylvania. Then a few days later, Nichole noticed Caleb wasn't as steady on his feet as he normally was; his equilibrium seemed off.

When Caleb's symptoms didn't subside, Nichole took him back to the doctor. Caleb's ears were still red and infected, reported the doctor, adding that a CAT scan would be ordered if he didn't improve in a few days. Nichole took her son home and hugged him close. She longed to hear his infectious laugh and see the twinkle in his brown eyes.

But five days later, Nichole's world changed forever. She was holding Caleb when he woke up, a blank stare on his face. "He wasn't looking at me, he was looking through me," Nichole remembered.

On the way to the hospital to seek medical help, "Caleb broke out in a horrible rash from head to toe and his body became stiff as a board," Nichole said. A CAT scan revealed Caleb had a brain tumor, and he was life-lifted to Children's Hospital of Philadelphia, where he underwent surgery to remove the tumor.

"The surgery was successful, but the tumor was malignant," said Nichole. "Caleb would need some form of radiation or chemotherapy, but we wouldn't know more until he opened his eyes."

But Caleb never woke up. Sadly, there was nothing more the doctors could do, and Nichole and her former husband prepared to take their son off life support. They took Caleb's hand- and footprints and gave him his last bath. They read to him, sang to him, and told him they loved him. Five days after his diagnosis, Caleb, cradled in his mother's arms, took his last breath.

Some months later—like signs from above—Nichole began finding pennies everywhere: pennies in the washing machine; pennies in a clean car. She'd walk by a spot, turn around and see a penny. "Do something," the little coins and Caleb seemed to be telling her, "something to help others."

And Nichole did. In May 2010, she launched Pennies from Heaven: Caleb's Foundation (www.calebspennies.org), a nonprofit that financially assists parents who otherwise couldn't afford to spend time with their critically ill children. "No parent should have to prioritize a payment or a job before the care of a sick child," explained Nichole, remembering the many children on Caleb's hospital ward who were all alone.

During its first three years, the foundation, which helps with mortgage and rent payments, utilities, car repairs, and other necessities, raised nearly $250,000 and assisted more than 210 families.

"Starting the foundation was my way of honoring Caleb's memory and keeping his beautiful spirit alive," said Nichole, adding that helping others is now a life passion.

Meanwhile, as Nichole continues to raise funds, pennies from heaven keep landing in her path. "I believe the pennies are little reassurances to keep going, to keep helping the families," said Nichole. "I can only hope Caleb is as proud of me as I am of him."

The Birthday Penny

How do you explain finding a penny while thinking about someone? Providence!

One year on February 11, Jean Marion, who lives in the American Southwest, was remembering her deceased father, Leo. It was his birthday, and while grocery shopping, she decided to celebrate his life with a bowl of cherry ice cream studded with chocolate chunks.

"How Dad loved chocolate-covered cherries!" Jean recalled. "He always received several boxes at Christmastime." As she headed toward the frozen foods aisle, her thoughts turned back in time to the wheat pennies she had saved as a kid.

"They don't make wheat pennies any more," her farmer-dad, who grew wheat and other crops on the Minnesota prairie, once told her. "Imaginative child that I was, I guarded my wheat pennies as though I owned all the gold in Fort Knox!" Jean laughingly said.

Her shopping done, Jean was unlocking her car door when she looked down. A penny! "I'm sure it wasn't there when I got out," she said, ex-

PENNY PRAYERS

plaining that she scans the ground like a searchlight for coins wherever she goes.

Jean picked up the penny, looked to heaven, and with a warm tear sliding down her cold cheek, began singing "Happy Birthday!" It was a sentimental but spiritual moment. "It was my dad's birthday," she said, "but I got the gift—a gift from heaven."

Pennies From Heaven

I found a penny today
Just lying on the ground
But it's not just a penny,
This little coin I've found.

Found pennies come from heaven
That's what my Grandpa told me.
He said angels tossed them down
Oh, how I loved that story!

He said when an angel misses you
They toss a penny down,
Sometimes just to cheer you up,
To make a smile out of a frown.

So don't pass by that penny
When you're feeling blue;
It may be a penny from heaven
That an angel's tossed to you.

Author unknown

Chapter Four

Pennies of Spirituality: In God We Trust to Increase Our Faith

Need a shot of faith? Turn to the penny! As the reflections in this chapter illuminate, a penny can lead us to trust more deeply, to be more attentive to others, and to know without a doubt that God is always there, always ready to pick us up. Inspecting a penny can also inspire prayer—and it won't cost you a cent.

A Penny and God's Listening Ear

What can the story of the widow's mite teach us? That God is always listening, always mindful of our needs, exhorts the Reverend John Keller, lead pastor of Resurrection Lutheran Church in Woodbury, Minnesota.

PENNY PRAYERS

I recently preached on the story of the widow's offering in Mark 12:41–44. The main point of my sermon was that Jesus noticed the widow's offering. He heard her drop two coins in the offering box and drew attention to her sacrificial gift. In a crowded, bustling temple courtyard, Jesus noticed a poor widow, someone whom the religious leaders seemed to ignore.

Jesus' observation gives me hope. In our complex, crowded, busy world, Jesus notices individuals, you and me. We are not simply some nameless creatures wandering the planet. We are not some number in a distant computer. We are a name, a face, a life to God. Our Creator knows our needs, our situations, the pleas of our hearts.

As part of my sermon, I had the congregation first listen to the sound of a large bag of coins filling a metal offering plate—the sound of the rich people. Then I had them listen to the soft clink of two copper coins. One had to listen carefully to hear the clink. How wonderful that Jesus heard.

I also invited the congregation to take a penny home and use it as a reminder of the widow's prayer. The penny reminds us that God is always listening and that our pleas will be heard. It is not a lucky penny, but a reminder of a loving God.

Adapted and reprinted with permission from Pastor Keller's blog at www.trustliveserve.wordpress.com.

Penny Blessings

"Trust in the LORD with all your heart, on your own intelligence do not rely" (Proverbs 3:5). For Diane Stahl Calcaterra of Coto de Caza, California, a found penny was the beginning of learning to trust anew.

As I walked back to the house something caught my eye: a mislaid penny. I usually find stray pennies on sidewalks and in parking lots. But in my own driveway? I reached down to pick it up.

The face of the coin was shiny and imprinted with the familiar phrase, "In God We Trust." I stopped and let the simplicity of those words sink in. How often do I start and finish my day doing just that? How often do I choose to trust God in the daily circumstances of my life?

Christian writer Sarah Young describes trusting God as a moment-by-moment choice. In her devotional book *Jesus Calling*, Young writes: "You trust Me when things go well, when you see Me working on your behalf. This type of trust flows readily within you, requiring no exertion of your will. When things go wrong...

[y]ou are forced to choose between trusting Me intentionally or rebelling....Having sacrificed My very life for you, I can be trusted in every facet of your life."

I brought that penny inside and placed it on my desk as a physical reminder of God's desire for me to trust in him. Sadly, I admit that my reliance on God has often been a last recourse as I collide with a crisis. But when I have turned to God, he has never let me down. Nope, not once! In fact, placing my trust in God always brought unexpected blessings in return. As I deliberately choose trust over despair, I'm receptive to the soothing and calm assurance that dependence on Christ can bring.

"In God We Trust"—four simple words on a penny that will bless your life!

Adapted and reprinted with permission from Diane Stahl Calcaterra's blog at www.familydevotionalblog.com.

Praying the Whole Penny

Just examining a penny can inspire prayer, explains the Reverend John Arnold, co-pastor of First Presbyterian Church of Texarkana, Arkansas, in this poignant mini-reflection.

One side of the penny has a person, Abraham Lincoln. This reminds us to pray for people. On the other side [of many pennies] is a place, the Lincoln Memorial, a reminder to pray for the "places" in our lives—churches, schools, homes, and places of work.

The penny has one more side: the edge. What challenges you? Stresses you out? Or puts you on edge? When we pray about our edges, we invite the Holy Spirit into our weakness. God can then pour his strength and miracle power into our weakness and begin transforming our lives.

Pray your pennies. Pray for people, pray for places, and pray your edges. It's a good way to bring change into your life!

Adapted and reprinted with permission from Reverend Arnold's blog at www.thepracticaldisciple.com.

Pennies for the Least of Our Brethren

After Father James Durkin of the Diocese of Camden, New Jersey, was ordained in 1968, he and classmate Father Brian O'Neill devised a found-penny program to help the "least of our brethren," a program that can be adopted by any penny-finder or Sunday-school class.

Whenever we saw a penny or any coin on the ground, we would pick it up and ask ourselves a few questions: How did it get there? How long has it been there? How many people passed by and either didn't pick it up or weren't interested in picking it up? How was I the one to find it and do something with it?

Then we would say several prayers, asking Jesus to forgive the sins of lost souls and to grant eternal rest to deceased souls. We also prayed for the homeless and gave glory to God for letting us find the coin and the opportunity to pray for a soul in need.

Over the past forty-five years, we have probably sent hundreds of dollars of found money to Mother Teresa's missions, Covenant House, and other charitable organizations with outreaches to the homeless and abandoned. Finding a penny and saying a prayer for the least of our brethren can change lives in more ways than we'll ever know.

Praying the Penny Forward

"See a penny, pick it up, and all day long you'll have good luck," the saying goes. Nancy Roberts of Woodbury, Minnesota, a prayer minister at her church, added a spiritual twist and turned it into a prayer—for others.

"Have a penny, give it away. Let someone else find it and have a good day," I'd rather say. I decided that if finding pennies made me so happy, why not scatter them for someone else to find? That began my quest of leaving a trail of penny prayers.

When I find a penny, I read the words "In God We Trust" and ask myself, *What should I be entrusting to you, Lord?* When someone or some situation comes to mind, I pray about it, give it to the Lord, and then leave the penny where someone else can find it. I've trusted God in the past, I'm trusting God in the here and now, and I'm praying it forward in the future.

Have you found a penny lately?

Pennies Are Like People

No two pennies are alike. Some pennies are shiny and new. Other pennies are tarnished and worn from age. As Florida resident Doug Spurling writes in this heartwarming reflection, pennies are a lot like people.

Have you ever found a penny? If so, listen. God is trying to tell you something.

One day around 1993, I found a penny. I picked it up. The next day I found another.

This started a routine that puzzled me. Without trying, without searching, I started

PENNY PRAYERS

finding a penny a day. At first, I thought it coincidence. After two weeks of finding a penny a day, I thought it weird.

I must be subconsciously trying to find these little rascals, I told myself.

So the next day I refused to look at the ground. Looking like a stuck-up snob, I walked around with my nose in the air. I did fine until mid-afternoon. After walking across the parking lot, nose in the air, I had to look down to open the truck door and—you guessed it. There on the ground, as pretty as a picture, lay a beautiful copper penny.

Now, after more than two weeks of penny finds, my lightning-fast brain figured, "If you can't beat 'em, join 'em." I started to pray. Each day after my daily penny find, I whispered: "Lord, are you trying to show me something?"

Day after day...penny after penny...prayer after prayer.

Suddenly, one day—after seeing, stopping, bending down, picking up, holding, and praying—it came to me.

"The Lord is close to the brokenhearted" (Psalm 34:19).

"The Lord God gathers the outcasts" (Isaiah 56:8).

"He heals the brokenhearted" (Psalm 147:3).

Then I heard this interior message:

"Those pennies have been cast aside.
Counted as nothing.
Many have been seen and stepped over.
Not counted as worthy enough to stoop down and pick up.
Many of My people are like those pennies.
In the same way I have given you eyes to see those pennies,
And the conviction to stoop down and pick them up.
I have given you eyes to see My people and
The conviction to pick them up."

I stopped seeing pennies that day—and started seeing people.

Have you found a penny lately? *Listen. God is trying to tell you something.*

Have you ever felt like a penny? God is near to pick you up.

Reprinted with permission from Doug Spurling's blog at http://dougspurling.blogspot.com.

The Lost Coin

Like coins, people also can be lost. In this reflection, Mary Kane of Michigan draws a parallel between the woman in the parable of the Lost Coin (Luke 15:8–10) who rejoices at finding the lost coin and God's finding us.

I am not a woman who is given to switching purses every time she changes her shoes. I have two basic purses: a summer purse (which is a small backpack) and a winter purse (which is black and has several compartments). Twice a year at the change of seasons, I clean out my purse and make the Big Switch.

I recently had Fall Purse Cleaning. Into the trash went all the old receipts, gum wrappers, and small bottles of lotion without caps. I also returned all the loose change, which continually escapes my wallet, to its rightful place. A few days later, while searching in my purse for a pen, I came across a penny that missed the Big Cleanup. I was about to drop the penny into the coin compartment of my wallet when I noticed it looked a little odd: the back of the penny was covered with peppermint bubble gum.

Without a second thought, I walked into the bathroom and tossed the sticky coin into the trash. As I threw the penny away, my grandfather came to mind. My hardworking, frugal German grandfather would have been horrified to know that I'd thrown away a penny.

When the woman in the parable of the Lost Coin discovered she was missing a coin, she also was horrified. "[W]hat woman having ten coins and losing one would not light a lamp and sweep the house, searching carefully until she finds it?" (Luke 15:8).

The lost coin was not worth very much, and the woman had nine more coins just like it. Why waste time looking for it? I would have been tempted to forget about the little coin (like my penny) and go shopping with the other nine. Though the coin was not valuable in and of itself, it was important to the woman who owned it.

The coins in this parable represent those who have yet to trust in Christ: small, lost, and insignificant, but very valuable to our heavenly Father. As each coin was valuable to the woman, every person is valuable to God. No one is a "throwaway penny."

How long did the woman search for the coin? Until she found it. And when she did, she gathered her friends and neighbors and said, "Rejoice with me because I have found the coin that I lost" (Luke 15:9).

I believe that as long as we draw breath, God will continue to pursue us, giving us opportunities to accept his gift of grace. God is longing for you to become *found*, for you to accept him as your Lord and Savior. And when you do, all heaven will rejoice over a "lost penny" that has been found.

Adapted and reprinted with permission from Mary Kane's article A Penny Saved *at www.onlybyprayer.com.*

God's Penny

Be careful what you pray for—even a penny—warns this humorous version of a well-known parable.

One day a preacher knelt down in his church and began to pray. "God," he asked, "how long is ten million years to you?"

"One second," God replied.

The preacher then asked, "God, how much is ten million dollars to you?"

"One penny," God replied.

With all the boldness the preacher could muster, he asked, "God, can I have one of your pennies?"

God replied, "Wait a sec."

Chapter Five

Penny Drives: In God We Trust for Impossible Projects

One penny alone has little power. But when tens of thousands of pennies are gathered together, the doors to the miraculous open. The impossible suddenly becomes possible. As the life-changing penny drives in this chapter illustrate, all it takes is a heavenly idea, a liberal dose of faith, and a few cents to get a miracle off and rolling.

French Pennies: Building the Frontier Church in America

What can a young French woman and a French penny do? Change the world for God! That's the amazing testimony of Pauline Marie Jaricot, who founded the Society for the Propagation of the Faith—and helped build the frontier Catholic Church in America.

Born in 1799, Pauline was the daughter of a silk merchant in Lyon, France, and lived in the lap of luxury. She was pretty, with warm eyes and dark hair, and was the belle of the ball in young Lyon society. Young ladies envied her, and young suitors fell head over heels for her. Pauline once confessed to having a new boyfriend every month!

At age fifteen, Pauline endured a heavy cross. She fell off a rickety stool and is thought to have severely injured her nervous system. Her ability to speak and walk was impaired, and she had to be watched so that she did not involuntarily hurt herself. Then her beloved mother died.

It took Pauline many months to recover from the traumas. When she finally rejoined the social scene, she no longer found it so appealing. Pauline heard an interior voice ask, *"When you are finished dancing, what good will it have done you?"* Her heart, she wrote at the time, was "made for the whole world," and she dreamed of "loving without end."

A Lenten sermon two years later sealed Pauline's conversion and mission in life. As Pauline sat in the pew, wearing an elegant blue taffeta dress and ornate Italian straw hat with roses, the priest preached about the sin of vanity and its manifestations in high-society women. Pauline's attire must have felt like a shackle. She immediately renounced her bourgeois lifestyle and began to dress in simple clothing and to attend to the sick and poor of Lyon, often at the hospital for incurables.

One day during prayer, Pauline, then eighteen years old, had a vision of two oil lamps, one empty, the other overflowing, the overflowing lamp filling up the empty one. To Pauline, the empty lamp signified the faith of France still reeling from the French Revolution. The overflowing lamp was the great faith of the Catholic missions, especially in the United States.

Give and it shall be given unto you, Scripture says. Pauline took that verse literally: She believed by giving to the missions, the oil of faith would return to France. (Pauline proved prophetic. Dozens of religious orders were founded in France during the nineteenth century; many of them went out into the world, some to the United States.)

In early 1818, Pauline made her first missionary appeal to 200 young women working at her brother-in-law's silk mill and gathered them into "circles of ten." Each member pledged to pray daily for the missions and to offer weekly a *sous*—a French penny—a great sacrifice for many workers. Members then recruited ten new members, and so on.

By 1822, Pauline had thousands of members enrolled to propagate the faith. Their pooled offerings were sent via the Paris Foreign Mission Society to Catholic missionaries in China. Back came letters of infant baptisms and adult conversions.

As Pauline's society grew, so did its reputation. In May 1822, a group of men in Lyon called *Les Messieurs* convened to discuss a financial appeal for American missions in Louisiana. The men were so impressed with the ingenuity and success of Pauline's society that they adopted her strategy. Shortly thereafter, *Les Messieurs* and Pauline united their efforts and collections for the universal good of the Catholic Church.

The first collection of the newly reorganized Society for the Propagation of the Faith in 1822 was divided between China and the United States—to the vast Diocese of Louisiana, which then extended from Florida to Louisiana, then north to Canada, and to the missions in Kentucky. During its first 100 years, the Society sent several million dollars to the frontier American Church, which was considered "mission territory" until 1908.

The Society was moved from France to Rome in 1922 and became the Vatican's official organization for providing missionary aid worldwide. In 1962, Pope John XXIII extolled Pauline's virtues and declared her "venerable," the first step toward sainthood. Today, the Society supports missions in more than 1,000 dioceses, mostly in Africa, Asia, and remote regions of Latin America.

Incredibly, it all began with a French penny and a young woman's heart as big as the world!

A Million Pennies for Dr. Kate

"If you would stop thinking about money and begin to have a little more faith, you would find that much more would be accomplished."

Pastor Radford's words echoed in Dr. Kate Newcomb's head. She smiled at the admonition, remembering how faith had built Boulder Junction Community Church in the early 1940s when there seemed to be no way. Dr. Kate bowed her head and, with a prayer on her lips and the trust of God in her heart, envisioned her hospital in tiny Woodruff, Wisconsin, finished and admitting patients.

What the country doctor couldn't envision was where the money would come from. But the good Lord had a plan: pennies—millions and millions of them.

Dr. Kate never intended to become a country physician. After graduating from medical school in 1917, she built up a flourishing practice in pediatrics and obstetrics in Detroit. When her husband, Bill, an autoworker, became deathly ill a few years later—the result of prolonged exposure to toxic fumes while working at a defense plant during World War I—they moved to the clean air of northern Wisconsin. She spent years nursing him back to health in the primitive bush, her medical career slipping away, along with memories of city life and modern conveniences: running water and electricity.

One blustery, snowy night in 1931, a local doctor telephoned Kate and demanded that she handle a medical emergency in her neck of the woods. He was thirty miles away, and the snow-drifted roads wouldn't be plowed until morning. Dr. Kate not only took the call, but she found her first love and was soon practicing medicine. Her "clinic" spanned 300 square miles of Wisconsin's north woods; house calls took her down every dirt road and forest trail and even across lakes in a canoe.

She doctored injured trappers and lumberjacks, sick Indians and homesteaders, sunburned campers and half-drowned vacationers.

When her car got stuck in the deep snow, she trekked by snowshoe to remote cabins to perform an emergency operation or deliver one of more than 3,000 babies by the light of a kerosene lamp. Nothing could stop the "angel on snowshoes," as she fondly came to be known.

It was a hardscrabble life in northern Wisconsin, and Dr. Kate never sent a bill. Her grateful patients paid her however they could: with chickens or venison, vegetables and wild berries, Indian moccasins or cordwood to heat her house in the biting cold winters.

In 1941, Dr. Kate opened her own clinic in Woodruff. Her hair graying and her step slowing, the fifty-six-year-old physician also began dreaming of her own hospital. It was becoming increasingly more difficult for her to treat patients in hospitals hundreds of miles away. One day Dr. Kate logged 376 miles making hospital calls across northern Wisconsin and into western Michigan.

In 1949, with a $1,000 check from a grateful vacationer Dr. Kate had treated, the hospital ball got rolling. The Lakeland Memorial Hospital board of directors was formed, and folks in Woodruff and nearby villages began holding spaghetti dinners, dances, anything to raise money. By 1952, the building fund totaled $50,000—$60,000 short of the estimated cost. Nevertheless, the hospital board decided to commence building, and in September 1952 the cornerstone was laid. The coffers dried up shortly thereafter, and construction stopped.

What seemed like the end to Dr. Kate was just the beginning. One day that fall at Arbor Vitae-Woodruff High School, Otto Burich was trying to illustrate to his geometry class how big a million is and suggested the class collect a million of something to understand the magnitude. "How about a million pennies?" one student asked. "A million pennies is $10,000!" another student piped in. "We can donate them to Dr. Kate's hospital."

And with that, the Million Penny Parade was born. In early November, students mailed out their first 500 letters asking for pennies. When newspapers and magazines began carrying stories of the penny drive, an avalanche began. Pennies rolled in by the wheelbarrows full, from forty-eight states and twenty-three countries. By April 1953, the students had met their goal: one million coppers—four and one-half tons of them!

On Memorial Day that year, the town of Woodruff celebrated with a Million Penny Parade. High-stepping majorettes led throngs of spectators to the high school gymnasium to view the mountain of pennies and to add even more one-centers to the pile. The final count was 1,700,000 pennies—or $17,000.

If Dr. Kate thought it was raining pennies from heaven, she had seen nothing yet.

When Ralph Edwards, host of the popular TV program *This Is Your Life*, caught wind of the Million Penny Parade to build Dr. Kate's hospital, he lured the doctor to California under the guise of her attending a medical convention. On March 17, 1954, a flabbergasted Dr. Kate found herself on national television.

"You're a legend in the great north woods, a figure of pioneer American living in our own day," said Edwards, adding that "you never enter a room without a prayer on your lips."

Twenty million Americans watched on TV as the hoax unfolded. One by one, the voices of family and patients told Dr. Kate's story as she remained in a daze. Edwards closed the story of Dr. Kate's life with the suggestion that viewers add their pennies to the fund for Lakeland Memorial Hospital and flashed her name and address on the screen.

Within days, sixty bags of mail had flooded the tiny Woodruff post office. One, ten, or dozens of pennies stuffed in envelopes. Piggy banks and cookie jars and shoeboxes filled to the brim with pennies. Thousands more envelopes carried checks or cash. When all the money had been counted, the total was a whopping $106,000—or 10,600,000 pennies!

It was more than enough money to complete the eighteen-bed hospital and furnish it with the latest medical equipment available. Lakeland Memorial Hospital was dedicated on July 21, 1954, and opened debt free.

To commemorate the Million Penny Parade, students at Arbor Vitae-Woodruff High School erected in 1954 the world's largest penny. Standing fifteen feet tall and weighing more than six tons, the Big Penny—like all pennies—proclaims the country's national motto. Above the bust of Abraham Lincoln in letters eight inches tall are the words "In God We Trust."

In 1988, the Dr. Kate Museum in Woodruff (www.drkatemuseum.org) was dedicated as a memorial to Dr. Kate and all the people who made Lakeland Memorial Hospital a reality. They trusted, and God provided—in a million more ways than one!

Feeding the Hungry With Pennies

Like the multiplication of the loaves and the fish, little is much in God's hands, especially pennies. In Vietnam, for example, four pennies can feed one hungry person—yes, just four pennies! And when everyone pools their pennies together, *millions are fed. That's the heartwarming story of Betty Swann's ministry, Pennies From Heaven. Like many outreaches, it began small—with $3.22, to be exact.*

The story begins in the fall of 2003, when the Amarillo, Texas, missionary began noticing stray pennies on the ground during walks with her friend, Sandra. Something prompted Betty to pick up the pennies and keep them in a jar. "I'm going to start saving these pennies and God will tell me what to do with them," Betty told Sandra.

Eighteen months later, in the spring of 2005, Betty began taking leadership teams of Christian men and women to Africa to help the Africans identify and use their specific God-given talents for his kingdom. While there, Betty heard firsthand accounts of corrupt officials stealing money and food that was intended for the starving masses. Thousands were dying. Betty's faith jumped into action, and she began sending donations to contacts in Africa she knew could be trusted to feed the hungry.

That December, Betty received an e-mail from a Member of Parliament in Malawi telling her of Malawi's terrible famine and later the floods that destroyed 8,000 homes in one district alone. Could Betty send help, big or little?

Betty solicited $2,000 for the small landlocked country in southeast Africa and then remembered the $3.22 in pennies and spare change that she had found. *I'll send that, too,* she thought.

A few weeks later, Betty had a heaven-cent idea: Why not ask other people to pick up pennies and donate them to feed the hungry? She e-mailed hundreds of friends and contacts about her plan, and they in turn sent the e-mail to their friends and so forth. Betty then opened a special account at Wells Fargo Bank so people could deposit their pennies at any of its branches nationwide. She also set up Pennies From Heaven as part of Betty Swann Ministries, a nonprofit, with every cent going to feed the hungry.

The pennies began rolling in. One woman gave a shoebox full of pennies. A homeless man donated two pennies. In San Diego, a Jewish woman whose life was spared during the Holocaust started a penny drive to save others. One penny pincher deposited twenty-four cents into Betty's bank account and another $82.88 (that's about a gallon and a half of pennies!). School classes caught the fever and held penny drives.

Like manna from heaven, the pennies began feeding the multitudes. Due to favorable exchange rates for American currency, meals cost about ten cents each in Malawi and Mozambique, as do meals in Pakistan and the Philippines, while meals in Belize and Mexico cost an estimated one dollar each.

"The least amount of money in the USA is the world to them," stated Betty, adding that the ministry's stringent accounting controls ensure all money is used to feed the hungry.

In early 2013, seven years after Betty began feeding the hungry, more than $150,000 (about $130,000 of that was pennies and spare change) has provided an estimated one million meals in twenty countries that also includes Egypt, Israel, Honduras, Haiti, Belarus, seven African nations, and Navajo Indians in the American Southwest.

While feedings in some countries were a one-time event, Betty's ministry has provided numerous feedings in Pakistan, where Christians are being persecuted and their homes burned down. The ministry also sends $1,500 monthly to help feed daily about forty orphans in Uganda and another 460 kids in Nairobi, Kenya. About eighty of the Kenyan children are orphans, while another 350 kids have single moms who work for minimum wage in the flower fields. Another thirty kids are street boys who eat like horses—or water buffalo! For about six cents each, the kids are fed meals of rice, cabbage, carrots, onions, and beans. Not only are the meals nutritious, they're tasty.

Once the children's bodies are nourished, academic and spiritual instruction can begin. The Kenyan government has recognized the head mother of the Nairobi orphanage, located in one of the city's worst slums, for mentoring and producing leaders. From the depths of poverty, the students are being raised up to go forth and serve their fellow human beings.

Even a lowly penny is much with God. His multiplication is like none other!

Pennies and spare change can be taken to any Wells Fargo Bank and deposited into the account of Betty Swann Ministries/Pennies From Heaven. Donations can also be mailed to Pennies From Heaven, P.O. Box 8882, Amarillo, TX 79114-8882 or made online at www.penniesfromheavenus.com.

Pennies of Hope

When twenty-two-year-old Christine Gianacaci of Hopewell Township, New Jersey, was killed in the massive earthquake that struck Haiti on January 12, 2010, her passion for helping kids didn't end—it began in a new way, one penny at a time.

"As a young girl, Christine was so outgoing that she earned the nickname 'the mayor,'" reminisced Jean Gianacaci, Christine's mother. "When a new student joined her class, Christine introduced herself and then introduced the new student to everyone else. She had a natural love for people and a contagious energy that was hard to contain."

At age eleven, Christine was diagnosed with Tourette syndrome, a neurological disorder that includes involuntary facial, motor, and vocal tics. Because of the constant ticking, Christine could no longer go to the movies, to church, or to other quiet places. She also endured ridicule and teasing from other kids, who never understood how much their words hurt. "The mayor" withdrew into her shell.

"On the inside, Christine was developing a pure understanding of the power of kindness and giving," said Jean. "When she was teased, she no longer got angry or resentful; instead, she tried to understand it. It became her signature trait always to be generous, even if nothing was given in return."

Toward the end of high school, the ticking subsided, and Christine enrolled at Lynn University in Boca Raton, Florida. During her sophomore year of college, Christine made her first mission trip—to Jamaica—and worked with kids living in extreme squalor. When Christine returned home, she talked of nothing else but making another mission trip. Christine was ministering to kids in Haiti when the earthquake took her life.

Turning tragedy into triumph, Christine's family founded Christine's Hope for Kids Foundation in late 2010. Just as Christine helped new kids in her class, the Foundation's "Pennies From Heaven" program has kids helping kids. At various schools, kids are filling gallon jars with pennies—one, two, ten pennies at a time. In the program's first two years, kids raised more than $9,000. One school alone amassed $2,800—that's 280,000 pennies!

Once the pennies are tallied, Christine's Hope for Kids Foundation, a nonprofit, matches the amount up to $3,000. Then the kids decide—with guidelines—where the money goes. "The kids are not only learning the value of money but also the social responsibility of helping the less fortunate," explained Jean.

Kids have awarded their pennies to worthy nonprofits such as "One Step Ahead Foundation," which helps children with physical disabilities build self-esteem and self-confidence through athletics, and "Spread the Magic Foundation," which stages magic shows to inspire hope and courage in children battling cancer.

Can one penny make a difference? Yes, if it's a penny of kindness and hope!

To learn more about Christine's Hope for Kids Foundation, visit www.christineshope.org.

The Legacy of Fifty-seven Cents

The faith of a little child can move mountains—and a church. That's the legacy of Hattie May Wiatt and a few cents.

In the mid-1880s, Hattie May and other children were standing with long faces outside Grace Baptist Church in Philadelphia, Pennsylvania. Like the main sanctuary—where tickets of admission were needed to get in—the Sunday school was packed to the rafters. There was no room for them to sit and hear the Word of God. Just then, Pastor Russell H. Conwell walked by and saw Hattie May. He scooped her up, carried her on his shoulders to the Sunday-school room, and found a chair for her in a dark corner.

The following day Pastor Conwell was walking to church when he met Hattie May. "When we get the money to erect a school building, we are going to construct one large enough to get all the little children in," Pastor Conwell told her, recalling the event during his sermon on December 1, 1912.

Hattie May began saving her money, but she became sick and died. At the funeral, Hattie's mother gave the pastor the little girl's gift of fifty-seven cents—no small sacrifice in those days. Deeply moved by the child's faith, Pastor Conwell, who founded Temple University and became wildly popular for his inspirational lecture *Acres of Diamonds,* announced to his flock what Hattie May had done.

"We have the first gift toward the new Sunday-school building," he said, teary-eyed.

As one story has it, Pastor Conwell changed the fifty-seven cents into fifty-seven pennies, sold them for a return of $250 (fifty-four of the pennies were returned to him), and used the proceeds to buy a nearby house for a Sunday school. Early classes of what would become Temple University were reportedly held here. Pastor Conwell later used the fifty-four returned pennies as the first payment on a lot where the congregation erected the legendary Baptist Temple.

"Almost 80,000 young people have gone through the classes of Temple University," continued Pastor Conwell's sermon in 1912, adding that in the university's first twenty years, an estimated 100 ministry students had graduated each year. "Think of it," he said, "2,000 people preaching the Gospel because Hattie May Wiatt invested her fifty-seven cents."

Hattie May's legacy continues to inspire people today. Give what you have—even the pennies she seems to be saying—and watch what the Almighty can do. Mountains will move, and great things can and will happen!

Penny Fact

"If a man could have started collecting a million pennies, a penny a day, on the day of the birth of Christ, he would complete his collection on about November 6, 2737."

From penny statistics compiled by students of Arbor Vitae-Woodruff High School in 1954.

Afterword

Praying the Nickel, Dime, Quarter, and Paper Bill, Too!

One Sunday, shortly after one of Marion Amberg's clients had departed this life, she was wondering where she'd find another client to replace her and the $600 in monthly income. Marion was walking to the Cathedral Basilica of St. Francis of Assisi in Santa Fe, New Mexico, when she found a nickel and a penny.

Six cents! Marion shouted inwardly, her heart thumping louder than the organ prelude inside. *What a cent-sational number!* She scooped up the coins and silently prayed, "God, I trust in you to provide the right client." A few days later, she found work for—you guessed it—$600 per month!

Coincidence?

"No, Providence!" said Marion. "Those six cents represented the $600 in lost income that I needed to replace."

The nickel is significant for another reason. If the U.S. Mint withdraws the penny from circulation as Canada and other nations have done (it reportedly costs the U.S. Mint two cents to make one cent), don't lose heart. You can also pray your nickels, dimes, quarters, and dollar bills. Every American coin and paper bill bears the words "In God We Trust." It's not the coin but the prayer that's important.

So pray your found coins, one by one, and be on the lookout for blessings from above. Who knows? You might receive a miracle!

To share your penny tale or to contact the author, send an e-mail to thepennyprayer@aol.com.